I Feel Depressed

Writing and designing by Zerarki Ayad
zerarki28ayad@gmail.com

ISBN: 9798374641691

Printed in the United States of America. First edition

Introduction

"Depression is a common and serious medical illness that negatively affects how you feel, the way you think, and how you act. It causes feelings of sadness and/or a loss of interest in activities once enjoyed. It can lead to a variety of emotional and physical problems and can decrease a person's ability to function at work and at home.[i] "

A wide range of research is being conducted on depression, from studies on the causes and risk factors for the condition to investigations into new treatments and therapies. "Some research focuses on understanding the underlying biology of depression, including the role of genetics and brain chemistry. [i]" Other research looks at the effectiveness of different types of psychotherapy, such as cognitive-behavioral therapy or talk therapy, and various medications used to treat depression. Additionally, research is being done on how depression can be prevented and how to support the best individuals living with depression.

It is important to note that depression is a highly individualized experience and that different people may have other causes, triggers, and treatment options that are effective for them. Research can help to provide a better understanding of depression and its effects, but it is essential to consult with a healthcare professional for personalized and appropriate treatment. It can lead to various emotional and physical problems and decrease a person's ability to function at work and at home.

In addition to biological and psychological research, there is also a growing body of research on social and environmental factors that can contribute to the development and maintenance of depression. This includes an analysis of the impact of stress, trauma, and adverse childhood experiences on mental health and studies on the role of social support and community resources in managing depression.

Research on depression is conducted in various settings, including universities, hospitals, and government agencies. Many studies are conducted using large samples of participants, such as those recruited through online platforms or from primary care clinics. Other studies may focus on specific subpopulations, such as veterans, older adults, or individuals from minority communities.

Many ongoing studies are trying to develop new treatments and therapies for depression, including new forms of psychotherapy, new medications, and technology such as virtual reality and app-based interventions. Studies are also being conducted to examine the potential benefits of complementary and alternative therapies, such as mindfulness, yoga, and acupuncture; it is also noted that the religious are less likely to be depressed.

Overall, research on depression is ongoing and multidisciplinary, aiming to understand the condition better and develop more effective ways to prevent and treat it. It is important to note that while research can provide valuable insights, it is always essential to consult with a healthcare professional for personalized and appropriate treatment.

A Journey Through Time: The Evolution of Understanding and Treating Depression

The history of knowledge about depression dates back to ancient civilizations, where descriptions of symptoms similar to those of depression can be found in texts from Egypt, Greece, and Rome. However, it wasn't until the 19th and 20th centuries that depression began to be understood as a specific medical condition.

In the late 19th century, the German psychiatrist Emil Kraepelin first used the term "depression" to describe a group of mental disorders characterized by low mood and loss of interest in activities.

Sigmund Freud, an Austrian neurologist and the founder of psychoanalysis, also contributed to the understanding of depression by describing it as a psychological condition caused by unresolved emotional conflicts.

In the 1930s, the Swiss psychiatrist Carl Jung introduced the concept of "complexes" to describe emotional and psychological experiences that can lead to depression.

In the 1950s and 1960s, researchers began to focus on the role of brain chemistry in the development of depression. The discovery of antidepressants, such as monoamine oxidase inhibitors (MAOIs) and tricyclic antidepressants (TCAs), marked a breakthrough in the treatment of depression.

In the 1980s and 1990s, research on depression continued to expand, with a focus on the effectiveness of various psychotherapies, such as cognitive-behavioral therapy (CBT) and interpersonal therapy (IPT), as well as new forms of antidepressant medication, such as selective serotonin reuptake inhibitors (SSRIs).

In recent years, there has been a growing interest in the role of inflammation and immune system dysfunction in the development of depression. Studies have also shown that epigenetic changes can play a role in the development of depression.

Overall, the knowledge about depression has developed over time through the contributions of many researchers and healthcare professionals across different fields. The understanding of depression as a complex and multifactorial condition has grown, and new treatments and therapies have improved the ability to manage this condition.

In recent years, research on depression has also begun to focus on the intersection of physical and mental health, recognizing that depression can be influenced by and can also influence other medical conditions such as heart disease, diabetes, and cancer. Studies on the impact of lifestyle factors, such as diet and exercise, on mental health have also gained momentum.

Research on depression has also begun to focus on how it affects different populations. For instance, studies have shown that people from minority communities, particularly African Americans and Latino Americans, may have higher rates of depression and may experience unique challenges in accessing mental health care. Research also indicates that depression is more prevalent among individuals who are LGBTQ+ and also among women.

Moreover, with the advent of technology and the increasing use of digital health tools, research on depression has begun to explore the potential benefits of telepsychiatry, mobile health apps, and virtual reality for assessing and treating depression.

It's important to note that despite the progress made in understanding depression and developing new treatments, much more research is needed to fully understand this complex condition and ensure that adequate care is available to all who need it.

In summary, the understanding and knowledge of depression have grown over time through the contributions of many researchers and healthcare professionals across different fields. Current research continues to explore new areas, such as the intersection of physical and mental health, the impact of lifestyle factors, the effect of depression on different populations, and the use of technology for assessment and treatment.

Definitions of depression

Depression is a mental disorder characterized by persistent feelings of sadness, hopelessness, and loss of interest in activities. It is also known as major depressive disorder or clinical depression, and it affects a person's thoughts, feelings, behavior, and physical health. Depression can range from mild to severe and can negatively impact a person's daily life and ability to function. "It is a common and serious medical illness that negatively affects how you feel, the way you think, and how you act.[i]"

Depression is a mental health condition characterized by persistent feelings of sadness, hopelessness, and loss of interest in activities. People with depression may also experience physical symptoms such as changes in appetite or sleep patterns. It can range from mild to severe and can negatively impact a person's daily life and ability to function. It is treatable with therapy, medication, or a combination of both.

Depression in the world now

Depression is a significant global health concern, affecting millions of people worldwide. "According to the World Health Organization (WHO), more than 264 million people of all ages suffer from depression.[i] " It is the leading cause of disability globally and significantly contributes to the overall global burden of disease.

In the United States, the National Survey on Drug Use and Health (NSDUH) reported that in 2020, an estimated 17.3 million adults aged 18 or older in the U.S. had at least one major depressive episode in the past year, representing 7.1% of all U.S. adults.

Research also shows that depression is more common in certain groups of people, such as women, people living in poverty, and individuals with chronic illnesses.

Depression can significantly impact a person's quality of life and lead to other health problems. It is a leading cause of absenteeism from work, and it is estimated that depression costs the global economy trillions of dollars each year in lost productivity.

However, many people do not receive the necessary treatment despite its prevalence and significant impact. According to WHO, only about 50% of people with depression worldwide receive treatment, and in low- and middle-income countries, this figure is even lower, at less than 25%.

Treatment for depression is available, including therapy, medication, and a combination of both. However, due to the stigma associated with mental health conditions, many people do not seek help. Therefore, increasing awareness of depression and reducing the stigma associated with it is crucial in ensuring that more people receive the treatment they need.

However, there may be differences in the prevalence, symptoms, and treatment of depression between Eastern and Western cultures.

In some Eastern cultures, depression may be viewed as a sign of weakness or a lack of willpower, leading to reluctance to seek help. Additionally, traditional Eastern medicine may emphasize herbal remedies and spiritual practices rather than Western-style psychiatric treatment.

On the other hand, Western cultures tend to view depression as a medical condition that requires professional treatment. Western medicine typically focuses on medication and psychotherapy as a treatment for depression.

According to a study published in the Journal of Affective Disorders, the prevalence of depression is generally higher in Western countries compared to Eastern countries. However, this may change as the stigma around mental health issues decreases, and more people seek help.

However, the symptoms of depression may differ between cultures. For example, somatic symptoms such as fatigue and headaches may be more prominent in some Eastern cultures. In contrast, emotional symptoms such as sadness and hopelessness may be more common in Western cultures.

It is important to note that depression is a complex condition that can vary significantly from person to person, regardless of cultural background. Therefore, healthcare professionals must consider cultural differences when diagnosing and treating depression.

It's important to note that these are generalizations, and individuals from any culture may have unique experiences and symptoms related to depression. It's also important to consider that the cultural context can change over time and across different regions.

Depression among men and women

Depression is a mental health condition that affects people of all genders. Still, research suggests that there may be some differences in the prevalence, symptoms, and treatment of depression between men and women.

According to the World Health Organization (WHO), depression is more common among women than men. In fact, studies have shown that women are nearly twice as likely to experience depression as men. This may be partly due to hormonal changes during a woman's menstrual cycle, pregnancy, and menopause. Additionally, women are more likely to experience certain life events that may increase the risk of depression, such as sexual abuse, domestic violence, and discrimination.

However, men are less likely to seek help for depression, and when they do, they may be less likely to be diagnosed with depression. This may be because men are more likely to externalize their emotions, such as by engaging in risky behavior or becoming aggressive, rather than expressing feelings of sadness or hopelessness.

Symptoms of depression can vary between men and women. For example, women are more likely to experience physical symptoms such as changes in appetite and sleep patterns, while men are more likely to experience irritability and anger. Men may also be more likely to engage in substance abuse as a way to cope with depression.

Treatment for depression is available and can include therapy, medication, and a combination of both. However, men may be less likely to seek help for depression and may also be less likely to adhere to treatment.

It's important to note that these are generalizations and individuals of any gender may have unique experiences and symptoms related to depression. It's also important to consider that gender identity and expression can vary greatly among individuals, and not all men or women will fit into the traditional stereotypes.

It is essential that healthcare professionals consider the unique experiences and needs of both men and women when it comes to diagnosing and treating depression. Additionally, raising awareness about depression among men and encouraging them to seek help is crucial in addressing this public health issue.

Causes of depression

Depression is a complex mental health condition that various factors can cause. Some of the most significant causes of depression include genetics, body shape, personality, and age.

Genetics plays a significant role in the development of depression. Studies have shown that people with a family history of depression are more likely to develop the condition themselves. This suggests that there may be a genetic component to depression, although the specific genes that may be involved are not yet fully understood.

Body shape may also be a factor in the development of depression. Research has shown that people who are overweight or obese are more likely to experience depression than those who are at a healthy weight. This may be partly due to the negative impact that being overweight or obese can have on a person's self-esteem and social interactions.

Personality can also play a role in the development of depression. People with certain personality traits, such as a tendency to be pessimistic or to ruminate on negative thoughts, may be more likely to experience depression than those who do not have these traits. Additionally, people who are highly sensitive to stress and have difficulty coping with difficult situations may be more at risk for depression.

Age is also a factor in the development of depression. Studies have shown that depression is more common among older adults, particularly those over 60. This may be due partly to the increased likelihood of experiencing stressful life events, such as the loss of a loved one or the onset of a chronic illness, as a person ages.

It's important to note that depression is a complex condition and that the causes can vary from person to person. A combination of genetic, environmental, and psychological factors can cause it. Additionally, it is essential to mention that depression is treatable with therapy, medication, or a combination of both.

In conclusion, depression is a complex mental health condition that can be caused by a variety of factors, including genetics, body shape, personality, and age. Understanding the causes of depression is crucial for developing effective treatments and reducing the stigma associated with this condition. Therefore, it is essential to consider all these factors when evaluating and treating depression in individuals.

Depression in pregnant and postpartum women

Depression is a significant concern among pregnant and postpartum women. "According to the World Health Organization (WHO), up to 20% of women experience depression during pregnancy or the year after giving birth, commonly known as postpartum depression.[i]"

During pregnancy, hormonal changes can trigger symptoms of depression, such as changes in mood, sleep patterns, and appetite. Women may also experience additional stressors during pregnancy, such as concerns about their baby's health or financial difficulties.

Postpartum depression, which occurs in the year after giving birth, is a more severe form of depression that can have a significant impact on a woman's ability to care for herself and her baby. Symptoms of postpartum depression can include feelings of sadness, hopelessness, anxiety, and fatigue.

"There are also other conditions related to postpartum such as postpartum anxiety, postpartum OCD, postpartum PTSD, and postpartum psychosis.[i]"

Risk factors for depression during pregnancy and postpartum include a history of depression or other mental health conditions, a lack of social support, financial difficulties, and a history of trauma or abuse.

It's important to note that untreated depression during pregnancy and postpartum can have a negative impact on both the mother and the baby. Depression can lead to poor prenatal care, low birth weight, and preterm birth. Additionally, depressed mothers may have difficulty bonding with their babies and may have trouble with breastfeeding and other aspects of caring for their newborns.

Effective treatment for depression during pregnancy and postpartum includes therapy, medication, or a combination of both. It's important to consult with a healthcare professional to determine the best course of treatment.

It's also important to note that support from family and friends and self-care activities such as exercise and healthy eating can help reduce the risk of depression during pregnancy and postpartum.

Therefore, it is important to be aware of the signs and symptoms of depression during pregnancy and postpartum and to seek help if you or someone you know is experiencing these symptoms. By providing early treatment and support, we can help to improve the outcomes for mothers and their babies.

Relationship of depression to alcohol or drug abuse

Depression and alcohol or drug abuse often co-occur and are referred to as a dual diagnosis or comorbidity. Individuals with depression may turn to alcohol or drugs to self-medicate and alleviate symptoms of depression. However, this coping can lead to the development of an addiction and worsen the symptoms of depression. Similarly, alcohol and drug abuse can lead to the development of depression due to changes in brain chemistry and the negative impact of substance use on mental health. Individuals with both depression and substance use disorder need to receive treatment for both conditions simultaneously to improve overall outcomes.

According to the National Survey on Drug Use and Health (NSDUH), in 2019, an estimated 20.8 million adults aged 18 or older in the United States had a substance use disorder. Of those, an estimated 8.1 million had both a substance use disorder and a mental illness, including depression.

Research has also shown that individuals with depression are more likely to develop an alcohol use disorder. A study published in the Journal of Affective Disorders found that individuals with major depression were 2.6 times more likely to develop alcohol dependence than those without depression.

Additionally, the National Institute on Alcohol Abuse and Alcoholism (NIAAA) states that alcohol use disorder is common among individuals with major depressive disorder, with estimates ranging from 20-30%.

Overall, it is clear that there is a strong relationship between depression and alcohol or drug abuse and that individuals with both conditions are at a higher risk for negative outcomes and require specialized treatment.

Relationship of work and social stress with depression

Work and social stress are both significant contributors to the development of depression. Stressful work environments can cause individuals to experience burnout, low job satisfaction, and lack of control over their work, which can lead to depression. Similarly, social stress can cause individuals to experience feelings of isolation, rejection, and lack of support, leading to depression.

Research has shown that individuals with high levels of work stress are at an increased risk of developing depression. A study published in the Journal of Occupational Health Psychology found that individuals with high levels of job strain (a combination of high demands and low decision latitude) had a 1.8 times greater risk of developing depression than those with low levels of job strain.

Similarly, social stress has been linked to depression. A study published in the Journal of Affective Disorders found that individuals with high levels of perceived social isolation had a 2.4 times greater risk of developing depression than those with low levels of perceived social isolation.

Overall, it is clear that work and social stress can contribute significantly to the development of depression and individuals need to manage these stressors effectively to maintain good mental health.

According to a study by the World Health Organization (WHO), about 264 million people globally suffer from depression. The study also found that work-related stress is a significant risk factor for the development of depression, with an estimated 12.5% of all cases of depression being attributed to occupational stress.

A survey by the American Psychological Association (APA) found that money and work were the top two sources of stress for Americans, with 72% of adults reporting that they were stressed about money at least some of the time and 69% reporting that they were stressed about work at least some of the time.

Another survey by Mental Health America (MHA) found that depression among people who identified as "overworked" is three times higher than among those who do not.

In terms of Social stress, a study by the Journal of Social Science & Medicine found that social isolation and loneliness increase the risk of premature death by 29%. The study also found that social isolation is as much a risk factor for early death as obesity and a more significant risk factor than physical inactivity or air pollution.

In conclusion, the relationship between work and social stress with depression is well established, and the statistics above show that it is a significant issue. Individuals need to be aware of the impact of these stressors on their mental health and take steps to manage them effectively.

Relationship of love and divorce with depression

Love and relationships can have a significant impact on mental health, particularly regarding depression. A lack of love and social support can contribute to feelings of isolation and rejection, which can lead to the development of depression. On the other hand, being in a happy and healthy relationship can provide individuals with a sense of security, companionship, and support, which can protect against the development of depression.

Divorce, in particular, can be a significant stressor that can contribute to the development of depression. The emotional and practical challenges of ending a marriage can be overwhelming, and losing a partner and social support can be especially difficult for some individuals. Research has shown that individuals who go through a divorce are at an increased risk of developing depression. A study published in the Journal of Affective Disorders found that individuals who had experienced divorce had a two-fold increased risk of developing depression compared to those who had never been divorced.

Overall, it is clear that love and relationships can significantly impact mental health and that ending a relationship through a divorce can be a significant stressor that can contribute to the development of depression. It is important for individuals going through a divorce to have access to support and resources to help them manage the emotional challenges of this experience.

According to a study by the American Psychological Association (APA), people who have gone through a divorce or separation are three times more likely to suffer from depression than those who are still in a relationship.

The study also found that divorced or separated individuals are more likely to have symptoms of depression than those who are widowed or never married.

Another study by the National Center for Biotechnology Information (NCBI) found that divorced individuals have higher rates of depression, anxiety, and substance abuse disorders than married individuals. The study also found that divorced individuals are more likely to have suicidal thoughts and attempts than married individuals.

Research also shows that divorce affects children and adolescents, leading to increased rates of depression, anxiety, and behavioral problems. A study by the journal of JAMA Pediatrics found that children whose parents divorced were at a higher risk of developing depression and anxiety symptoms than those whose parents remained married.

In conclusion, The statistics above clearly show that divorce is a significant stressor that can contribute to the development of depression and other mental health issues. Individuals going through a divorce to have access to support and resources needed to help them manage the emotional challenges of this experience, and children to be provided with support to mitigate the effects of the divorce.

Relationship of self-satisfaction with depression

Self-satisfaction, also known as self-esteem, can have a significant impact on mental health, particularly concerning depression. Individuals with low self-esteem may feel a sense of worthlessness, inadequacy, and helplessness, which can lead to the development of depression. On the other hand, individuals with high self-esteem may have a sense of self-worth, competence, and control, which can protect against the development of depression.

Research has shown that individuals with low self-esteem are at an increased risk of developing depression. A study published in the Journal of Affective Disorders found that individuals with low self-esteem had a three-fold increased risk of developing depression compared to those with high self-esteem.

Additionally, a study by the Journal of Social Psychology found that self-esteem is inversely related to depression, meaning that as self-esteem increases, depression decreases and vice versa.

Moreover, self-esteem can also play a role in recovery from depression. A study published in the Journal of Clinical Psychology found that individuals with higher self-esteem had better outcomes in treatment for depression and were more likely to maintain their recovery over time.

Overall, it is clear that self-satisfaction or self-esteem can have a significant impact on mental health, particularly regarding depression. Individuals with low self-esteem are at an increased risk for developing depression, and those with high self-esteem are more likely to recover from depression and maintain recovery over time. Individuals with low self-esteem need to work on improving their self-worth while at the same time seeking professional help if they are suffering from depression.

According to a Journal of Social Psychology study, people with low self-esteem are more likely to experience depression. The study found that individuals with low self-esteem had a three times greater risk of developing depression than those with high self-esteem.

Another study by the Journal of Clinical Psychology found that people with low self-esteem tend to have a higher risk of depression and anxiety and that people with high self-esteem have a lower risk of depression and anxiety.

A study by the journal JAMA Psychiatry found that individuals with low self-esteem had an increased risk of depression and anxiety and that these associations were stronger in women than in men.

In addition, A study by the National Institutes of Mental Health (NIMH) found that people with low self-esteem were more likely to experience depression, anxiety, and other mental health issues. The study also found that people with low self-esteem had a more challenging time recovering from these conditions and were more likely to relapse.

In conclusion, the statistics above clearly show a strong relationship between self-satisfaction or self-esteem and depression. People with low self-esteem have a greater risk of developing depression and have a more challenging time recovering from depression. Individuals with low self-esteem need to work on improving their self-worth while seeking professional help if they suffer from depression.

Depression in veterans

Depression is a common mental health condition among veterans. It is estimated that around 20% of veterans who served in recent conflicts, such as Operation Iraqi Freedom (OIF) and Operation Enduring Freedom (OEF), have experienced depression.

Veterans who have experienced combat or have been exposed to traumatic events while serving are at a higher risk of developing depression. Trauma can take many forms, including physical injury, sexual assault, and exposure to violence or death. These experiences can lead to the development of post-traumatic stress disorder (PTSD), which is a strong risk factor for depression.

The symptoms of depression among veterans may differ from those seen in the general population, as veterans may be more likely to experience physical symptoms such as chronic pain and fatigue. In addition, veterans may also be at a higher risk for substance abuse and suicide, as they may turn to alcohol or drugs to cope with depression and other mental health conditions.

Veterans need to receive appropriate mental health care in order to manage the symptoms of depression and other mental health conditions. Treatment options for depression include medication, psychotherapy, and support groups. The

Department of Veterans Affairs (VA) provides mental health care services to veterans, including treatment for depression.

Overall, depression is a common issue among veterans, especially those exposed to trauma. It is essential for veterans to have access to appropriate care and support to manage the symptoms and improve their mental health.

Winter depression

Winter depression, also known as seasonal affective disorder (SAD), is a type of depression that occurs at the same time every year, typically during the winter months. It is characterized by symptoms of depression such as feelings of sadness, hopelessness, and a lack of interest or pleasure in activities, as well as changes in sleep, appetite, and energy levels.

The exact cause of SAD is unknown, but it is believed to be related to changes in the amount of sunlight that a person is exposed to during the winter months. The shorter days and longer nights of winter can disrupt the body's internal clock, leading to changes in mood and other symptoms of depression.

Risk factors for SAD include living in a location with long, dark winters, having a family history of SAD, and having a history of major depression. Women are more likely than men to develop SAD, and younger people are more likely to develop SAD than older adults.

Treatment options for SAD include light therapy, medication, and psychotherapy. Light therapy involves sitting in front of a special light box that emits bright light for a specific amount of time each day. Medications such as antidepressants may also be prescribed to help manage the symptoms of SAD.

It is essential for individuals who think they may have SAD to seek help from a healthcare professional. If untreated, SAD can lead to more severe depression and interfere with daily activities. With proper treatment, the symptoms of SAD can be managed, and individuals can lead an everyday life during the winter months.

Functional depression

Functional depression, also known as dysthymia or persistent depressive disorder, is a type of depression that is characterized by a low-grade, chronic depression that lasts for at least two years. Unlike major depression, which can cause severe symptoms that interfere with daily activities, functional depression is characterized by milder symptoms that may be more difficult to recognize.

Symptoms of functional depression include:

- Persistent feelings of sadness or hopelessness.
- Lack of interest or pleasure in activities.
- Low self-esteem or self-worth.
- Difficulty sleeping or oversleeping.
- Fatigue or loss of energy.
- Difficulty concentrating or making decisions.
- Recurrent thoughts of death or suicide.

Individuals with functional depression may not experience all of the symptoms of major depression. However, they may still experience significant impairment in their ability to function in their daily lives. They may have difficulty with work, school, or maintaining relationships and may struggle with feelings of worthlessness and hopelessness.

Functional depression is often overlooked because the symptoms are not as severe as those of major depression and may be mistaken for normal sadness or stress. Individuals need to seek help from a healthcare professional if they think they may have functional depression, as if left untreated, it can lead to more severe depression. It can also cause a chronic and debilitating condition.

Treatment options for functional depression include psychotherapy, medication, and self-care strategies such as regular exercise, healthy eating, good sleep habits, and stress management. With the proper treatment, it is possible to manage the symptoms of functional depression and improve overall well-being.

Symptoms of depression

Depression, also known as major depressive disorder, is a mental health condition characterized by persistent feelings of sadness, hopelessness, and a lack of interest or pleasure in activities. It can manifest in different forms and severity levels.

Major depression, also known as clinical depression, is characterized by a combination of symptoms that interfere with a person's ability to work, sleep, study, eat, and enjoy once-pleasurable activities. Some of the symptoms of major depression include:

- Persistent feelings of sadness, hopelessness, or emptiness.
- Loss of interest or pleasure in activities that were once enjoyed.
- Significant changes in weight or appetite.
- Difficulty sleeping or oversleeping.
- Physical agitation or slowing.
- Fatigue or loss of energy.
- Feelings of worthlessness or guilt.
- Difficulty concentrating or making decisions.
- Recurrent thoughts of death or suicide.
- Low self-esteem or self-worth.

Mild depression, also known as dysthymia or persistent depressive disorder, is a less severe form of depression characterized by symptoms that are not as severe as those of major depression but still interfere with a person's ability to function normally.

It's important to note that the above symptoms should be present for at least two weeks before a diagnosis of depression can be made. Also, these symptoms are not unique to depression and should be evaluated by a mental health professional to rule out other possible causes.

Types of depression

There are several different types of depression, each with its symptoms and causes. Some of the most common types include:

1- Major depressive disorder is the most severe type of depression and is characterized by persistent feelings of sadness, hopelessness, and a loss of interest or pleasure in activities. Other symptoms may include changes in appetite and sleep patterns, fatigue, difficulty concentrating, and thoughts of suicide or self-harm.

2- Persistent depressive disorder (Dysthymia): This is a chronic form of depression that lasts for at least two years. A persistent low mood, feelings of hopelessness, and a lack of interest or pleasure in activities characterize it. The symptoms are less severe than those of major depression but are still present for a significant time.

3- Postpartum depression: This type of depression occurs in women after giving birth. Feelings of sadness, hopelessness and a lack of interest or pleasure in activities characterize it. It may also include feelings of guilt or worthlessness, appetite and sleep patterns changes, and difficulty bonding with the baby.

4- Seasonal affective disorder (SAD): This type of depression is associated with changes in seasons and typically occurs during the fall and winter months. Feelings of sadness, hopelessness and a lack of interest or pleasure in activities characterize it. It may also include changes in appetite and sleep patterns, fatigue, and difficulty concentrating.

5- Bipolar disorder: This type of depression is characterized by episodes of mania (abnormally elevated or irritable mood) and depression. It's also known as manic-depressive disorder.

It's important to note that these types of depression are not mutually exclusive, and a person may have symptoms of more than one type of depression at the same time. A professional evaluation is necessary for an accurate diagnosis and treatment.

Brain chemistry and depression

Depression is thought to be caused by a combination of factors, including genetics, brain chemistry, and life events. Brain chemistry plays a significant role in the development of depression.

Research has shown that people with depression have changes in the levels of certain chemicals in the brain called neurotransmitters. These chemicals help transmit signals between nerve cells in the brain. Specifically, the levels of serotonin, norepinephrine, and dopamine, which are known to play a role in regulating mood, are often low in people with depression.

The exact cause of these changes in brain chemistry is not well understood, but it's thought that a combination of genetic, environmental, and psychological factors may be involved. Some research suggests that stress can cause changes in the brain that lead to depression.

Treatment for depression often involves medication or therapy that aims to correct these imbalances in brain chemistry. Antidepressant medications, for example, work by increasing the levels of certain neurotransmitters in the brain. Therapy, specifically cognitive behavioral therapy, can help individuals challenge negative thoughts and change negative behavior patterns.

It's important to note that depression is complex and multifactorial, and even though brain chemistry is involved, it's not the only cause of depression. Different people may have different causes and triggers.

Sadness and psychological trauma are closely related to depression, as they can both contribute to the development of the condition.

Sadness is a normal human emotion that a wide range of events, such as the loss of a loved one, the end of a relationship, or disappointment, can cause. It is usually short-lived and can be resolved with time and support. But, when sadness persists and interferes with a person's ability to function, it can lead to depression.

Psychological trauma, such as experiencing or witnessing a traumatic event, can also contribute to the development of depression. Trauma can cause significant changes in the brain, including changes in the levels of neurotransmitters, which can lead to depression. Trauma can also lead to the development of negative beliefs about oneself and the world, which can further contribute to depression.

Both sadness and trauma can affect a person's ability to cope with daily life, causing them to feel overwhelmed and hopeless. This can lead to a lack of interest in activities and a lack of motivation. It can also lead to changes in sleep and eating patterns, fatigue, and difficulty concentrating.

It's important to note that the relationship between sadness, trauma, and depression is complex, and not everyone who experiences sadness or trauma will develop depression. But, those who do will need professional help to overcome it. A combination of therapy and medication, as well as self-care, can help alleviate symptoms and promote healing.

The difference between sadness and depression

Sadness and depression are two distinct emotional states, although they share some similarities. The main difference between the two is the duration and intensity of the feelings.

Sadness is a normal human emotion that everyone experiences at some point. It is a natural response to challenging or distressing events, such as losing a loved one, breaking up, or disappointment. Sadness usually passes relatively quickly and is manageable with the support of loved ones and time.

Depression, on the other hand, is a mental health disorder characterized by persistent feelings of sadness, hopelessness, and a loss of interest in activities. Depression affects one's mood, thoughts, feelings, and physical well-being. It is a severe and persistent feeling of sadness that interferes with daily life.

Symptoms of depression can include changes in appetite, sleep patterns, energy levels, self-esteem, difficulty concentrating, feelings of guilt or worthlessness, and thoughts of suicide. These symptoms are often chronic or recurrent and can last for weeks, months, or even years.

It is important to note that depression can manifest differently in different individuals and can be accompanied by other symptoms such as anxiety, irritability, and lack of motivation.

In summary, while sadness is a normal emotion everyone experiences, depression is a severe mental health condition that requires professional attention. If you or someone you know is experiencing symptoms of depression, it is essential to seek help from a healthcare professional.

Sadness	Depression
A typical reaction to losses.	Satisfactory condition.
The sadness may be temporary, and the person can still enjoy other things and look forward to the future.	The sadness continues, and the person cannot enjoy nor think positively about the future.
The person still maintains his self-confidence.	Feelings of inferiority are common.

Depression treatment

Treating depression with medication is a common and effective approach for managing the symptoms of depression. Antidepressant medications, also known as psychotropics, work by affecting the levels of certain chemicals in the brain, known as neurotransmitters, which are involved in regulating mood.

Several different types of antidepressant medications are commonly used to treat depression, including:

1- Selective serotonin reuptake inhibitors (SSRIs): These medications work by increasing the levels of the neurotransmitter serotonin in the brain. They are considered the first-line treatment for depression and are generally well-tolerated with few side effects. Some examples of SSRIs include fluoxetine (Prozac), sertraline (Zoloft), and paroxetine (Paxil).

2- Serotonin and norepinephrine reuptake inhibitors (SNRIs): These medications work by increasing the levels of both serotonin and norepinephrine in the brain. They are considered the second-line treatment for depression and are generally well-tolerated. Some examples of SNRIs include venlafaxine (Effexor) and duloxetine (Cymbalta).

3- Tricyclic antidepressants (TCAs): These medications work by increasing the levels of both serotonin and norepinephrine in the brain. They are considered less preferred than SSRIs and SNRIs because of their side effects, such as dry mouth, blurred vision, constipation, and drowsiness. Examples of TCAs include amitriptyline (Elavil) and imipramine (Tofranil).

4- Monoamine oxidase inhibitors (MAOIs): These medications work by inhibiting the activity of the enzyme monoamine oxidase, which breaks down the neurotransmitters serotonin, norepinephrine, and dopamine. They are considered less preferred than SSRIs, SNRIs, and TCAs because of the dietary restrictions and potential for dangerous interactions with certain foods and medications. Examples of MAOIs include phenelzine (Nardil) and tranylcypromine (Parnate)

It's important to note that it may take several weeks or even months before the full benefits of antidepressant medications become apparent, and it may take some time to find the proper medication and dosage. Also, it's important to continue taking medication as prescribed, even if symptoms improve, to prevent relapse.

It's also important to note that medication should be used in conjunction with therapy and other forms of treatment, such as self-care, to help manage symptoms of depression.

Additionally, patients should be monitored by a mental health professional to ensure the medication is effective and safe and that any potential side effects are managed.

Treatment of depression through sessions or groups is a common and effective approach for managing the symptoms of depression. Several different types of therapy can be used, each with its unique approach.

1- Cognitive Behavioral Therapy (CBT): This type of talk therapy focuses on helping individuals change negative patterns of thought and behavior. It aims to identify and change negative beliefs and ideas contributing to depression and teach coping strategies to manage symptoms.

2- Interpersonal therapy (IPT): This therapy focuses on helping individuals improve their relationships and social support. It aims to address interpersonal issues that contribute to depression, such as difficulties in communication and problem-solving, and to improve the quality of the patient's relationships.

3- Psychodynamic therapy: This therapy focuses on helping individuals understand the underlying emotional and psychological issues that contribute to depression. It aims to uncover unconscious thoughts and feelings that may be contributing to depression and to help the patient to understand and process those thoughts and feelings.

4- Group therapy: This type of therapy involves a group of people who are dealing with similar issues, such as depression. It can be a powerful tool for individuals to share their experiences and to receive support and feedback from others. Group therapy can also provide a sense of belonging and can be beneficial for people who may feel isolated or lonely.

5- Support groups: Support groups are a type of therapy that focuses on providing emotional and social support. They are often led by a trained facilitator and allow individuals to share their experiences and feelings and to receive support and guidance from others who are going through similar experiences.

It's important to note that different people may respond differently to varying types of therapy, and it may take some time to find the right therapy for an individual. It's also important to note that therapy should be used with medication and other forms of treatment, such as self-care, to help manage symptoms of depression. A mental health professional can help determine the best course of treatment for an individual based on their specific needs and circumstances.

Depression is a mental health disorder characterized by persistent sadness, hopelessness, and a loss of interest in activities. To diagnose depression, a healthcare professional will typically conduct a thorough assessment, including a physical examination, laboratory tests, and a psychological evaluation.

1- Psychological evaluation: A healthcare professional will typically conduct a psychological evaluation to assess the presence and severity of symptoms of depression. This may include a clinical interview, in which the healthcare professional will ask questions about the individual's mood, thoughts, and behavior, and may also include standardized questionnaires or self-report measures.

2- Physical examination: A physical exam may be conducted to rule out any underlying medical conditions that could be contributing to the individual's symptoms.

3- Laboratory tests: Laboratory tests, such as blood tests, may be conducted to rule out any underlying medical conditions that could be contributing to the individual's symptoms.

4- Diagnostic criteria: The healthcare professional will use the Diagn standards of The Diagn and Statistical Manual of Mental Disorders (DSM-5) or the International Statistical Classification of Diseases and Related Health Problems (ICD-10) to make the diagnosis of depression, which requires the presence of specific symptoms in a particular period.

It is important to note that depression is a complex disorder, and a variety of factors may contribute to its development. Therefore, it is essential to work with a qualified healthcare professional to diagnose and treat depression accurately.

Ways to prevent depression

Depression is a severe mental health condition that can significantly impact an individual's quality of life. While it is not always possible to prevent depression, several things can be done to reduce the risk of developing the condition or to manage symptoms if they do occur. Some ways to prevent depression include:

1- Exercise regularly: Regular physical activity has been shown to improve mood and reduce symptoms of depression. Aim for at least 30 minutes of moderate-intensity exercise most days of the week.

2- Maintain a healthy diet: Eating a balanced diet rich in fruits, vegetables, and whole grains can help improve mood and reduce the risk of depression.

3- Get enough sleep: Getting adequate sleep is essential for maintaining good mental health. Aim for 7-9 hours of sleep per night.

4- Build and maintain social connections: Strong social connections can provide support and a sense of belonging, which can help to reduce the risk of depression.

5- Manage stress: Stress can trigger or worsen depression. Finding healthy ways to manage stress is important, such as yoga, meditation, or therapy.

6- Seek professional help: If you are experiencing symptoms of depression, it is important to seek professional help. This can include therapy, counseling, or medication.

7- Identify and address negative thinking: Negative thoughts and beliefs can contribute to depression. It is essential to be aware of negative thoughts and to challenge and change them.

It is important to remember that depression is a treatable condition, and with the proper support, people can recover and lead fulfilling lives.

- When starting to use the medication:

Some of them suffer from suicidal thoughts, especially those under the age of twenty-five; Therefore, they should be closely monitored, especially at the beginning of using medications, or when changing doses.

- It would be best to talk to the doctor before using medications during pregnancy, when planning a pregnancy, or before breastfeeding about the effect of drugs on the mother and the child.

- The danger of stopping medicines suddenly: You should not stop using drugs suddenly, without telling the doctor, not because they may cause addiction, but because the body is accustomed to them. Therefore, it must be withdrawn from the body gradually, under a specialist doctor's observation. To avoid withdrawal symptoms.

Depression and suicide

Depression is a serious mental illness that can lead to suicide. Suicide is intentionally causing one's death and is a leading cause of death worldwide. People with depression are at a higher risk of suicide than the general population.

Depression causes feelings of hopelessness, helplessness, and worthlessness, which can lead individuals to believe that suicide is the only solution to their problems. They may also experience a loss of interest in activities, changes in sleep and eating patterns, and feelings of guilt and shame. These symptoms can make it difficult for individuals to see a way out of their suffering, and they may turn to suicide as a means of escape.

It's important to note that suicide is preventable, and early intervention is key. If you or someone you know is experiencing symptoms of depression or is showing signs of suicide, it's essential to seek help immediately.

There are several warning signs that someone may be considering suicide, including:

- Talking about wanting to die or kill oneself.
- Expressing feelings of hopelessness or helplessness.
- Talking about feeling trapped or in unbearable pain.
- Talking about being a burden to others.
- Increasing alcohol or drug use.
- Acting anxious or agitated.
- Withdrawing from friends, family, and activities.
- Changing eating and sleeping habits.
- Giving away prized possessions.

- Saying goodbye to people as if it were for the last time.

If you or someone you know is experiencing these symptoms, it's important to seek help immediately. Some resources available include:

- National Suicide Prevention Lifeline: 1-800-273-TALK (8255).
- Crisis Text Line: Text "HELLO" to 741741.
- Local emergency services: dial 911.

It's important to remember that depression and suicidal thoughts are treatable, and with the right help, individuals can recover and lead happy and fulfilling lives.

Depression is also closely linked to suicide. According to the American Foundation for Suicide Prevention (AFSP), suicide is the 10th leading cause of death in the U.S., and there are an estimated 121 suicides per day. In 2019, the suicide rate was 14.0 per 100,000 individuals. Suicide is also more common among men than women, with men being 3.5 times more likely to die by suicide than women.

It's important to note that depression and suicide are preventable and early intervention is key. With the right help, individuals with depression can recover and go on to lead happy and fulfilling lives. People need to seek help if they are experiencing symptoms of depression or suicidal thoughts and to be aware of the resources available to them, such as the National Suicide Prevention Lifeline and Crisis Text Line.

Complications of depression

Depression is a serious mental health condition that can lead to several complications if left untreated. Some of the most common difficulties of depression include:

- Suicidal thoughts and behavior: Depression is a major risk factor for suicide, and individuals with depression may have thoughts of ending their own lives or may attempt suicide.

- Substance abuse: Individuals with depression may turn to drugs or alcohol as a way to cope with their symptoms, which can lead to addiction and further complications.

- Physical health problems: Depression can lead to several physical health problems, such as heart disease, diabetes, and stroke.

- Difficulty functioning in daily life: Depression can make it difficult for individuals to carry out normal day-to-day activities, such as going to work or school, caring for loved ones, and maintaining relationships.

- Chronic depression: Long-term depression can lead to chronic depression, which can cause severe symptoms and make it difficult to recover.

- Other mental health disorders: Depression may also increase the risk of developing other mental health disorders, such as anxiety disorder and bipolar disorder.

It is important to seek professional help if you or someone you know is experiencing symptoms of depression. With proper treatment, the complications of depression can be minimized or prevented.

Effects of depression on the cardiovascular and immune systems

Depression has been shown to have several negative effects on both the cardiovascular and immune systems.

Regarding cardiovascular health, depression has been linked to an increased risk of heart disease, stroke, and high blood pressure. This may be partly because individuals with depression often engage in unhealthy behaviors, such as smoking and physical inactivity, which can increase the risk of cardiovascular disease. Additionally, depression has been associated with increased levels of inflammation in the body, which can contribute to the development of heart disease.

Depression also appears to have a negative impact on the immune system. Studies have shown that individuals with depression have lower levels of specific immune cells, such as T-cells and natural killer cells, which play a key role in fighting infection and disease. Additionally, depression has been linked to an increased risk of developing certain autoimmune disorders, such as rheumatoid arthritis and lupus.

It's important to note that depression can also result from chronic illness and that the relationship between depression and the cardiovascular and immune systems is bidirectional.

Overall, depression appears to have several negative effects on the cardiovascular and immune systems. Individuals with depression must seek treatment to improve their health and well-being.

Depression and sexual health

Depression can have a significant impact on sexual health. People with depression may experience a loss of interest in sexual activity, also known as sexual dysfunction. Both physical and psychological factors can cause this. Depression can lead to hormone changes, affecting sexual desire and function. Additionally, depression can cause low self-esteem, guilt, and worthlessness, making it difficult for an individual to engage in sexual activity.

Depression can also negatively impact sexual function in both men and women. Men may experience erectile dysfunction, and women may experience problems with lubrication or sexual desire. Additionally, depression can lead to decreased sexual desire and satisfaction and reduced ability to orgasm.

It's worth mentioning that depression can also be a side effect of some medications used to treat sexual dysfunction, such as antidepressants, which can further complicate the issue.

It's important to note that depression and sexual dysfunction can be treated together by a healthcare professional. Therapy, such as cognitive-behavioral therapy, can help individuals with depression improve their mood and self-esteem, improving their sexual function. Medications used to treat depression may also be used to treat sexual dysfunction. Additionally, lifestyle changes, such as exercise, a healthy diet, and stress management, can help improve sexual health and overall well-being.

Overall, depression can significantly impact sexual health, and it's essential for individuals with depression to seek treatment to improve their sexual function and overall well-being.

Research has shown a strong relationship between depression and sexual health.

A study published in the Journal of Sexual Medicine found that among individuals seeking help for sexual dysfunction, 43.1% met the criteria for depression. Additionally, a study published in the Journal of Affective Disorders found that among individuals with depression, 43.8% reported sexual dysfunction.

Another study published in the Journal of Clinical Psychiatry found that among individuals with major depressive disorder, 71.4% reported experiencing sexual dysfunction.

Additionally, a study published in the Journal of Psychiatric Research found that among individuals with depression, sexual dysfunction was reported in 57% of men and 43% of women.

These statistics demonstrate a strong relationship between depression and sexual health and highlight the importance of addressing both issues when treating patients.

It's worth noting that these studies have different sample sizes, different population characteristics, and different definitions of sexual dysfunction, which can affect the results and conclusion.

Overall, these statistics provide evidence of the significant impact that depression can have on sexual health, highlighting the importance of addressing both issues when treating patients.

Masked depression

Masked depression, also known as "smiling depression," is a type of depression in which a person may appear to be functioning well on the outside but is struggling with feelings of sadness and hopelessness on the inside. This can make it difficult for friends, family, and even mental health professionals to recognize the signs of depression, as the person may not exhibit typical symptoms such as crying or feeling hopeless.

Individuals who have masked depression may be able to put on a "happy face" and continue with their daily activities. Still, they may struggle with worthlessness, guilt, and helplessness. They may also have physical symptoms such as fatigue, headaches, and changes in appetite.

It is important to note that masked depression is not a distinct mental health disorder but rather a way to describe a pattern of depression that can be difficult to recognize. It's essential to seek help from a mental health professional if you or someone you know is struggling with depression, regardless of whether it appears to be masked.

Treatment for masked depression typically involves a combination of therapy and medication. Cognitive-behavioral therapy (CBT) and interpersonal therapy (IPT) are two effective types of therapy in treating depression. Antidepressant medications, such as selective serotonin reuptake inhibitors (SSRIs), may also be prescribed to help alleviate symptoms of depression.

It's important to note that it's not uncommon for people to hide their true feelings and struggles. Hence, it's always important to take care of ourselves and each other by being aware of how we feel and being open to listening and supporting loved ones.

The fear of death, also known as thanatophobia, can be a significant factor in the development of depression. People afraid of death may experience various emotional and psychological symptoms, such as anxiety, sadness, and hopelessness. This fear can also lead to isolation and a lack of motivation to engage in activities that were once enjoyed.

Depression and the fear of death can also have a cyclical relationship. Depression can lead to feelings of helplessness, hopelessness, and a lack of purpose, which can exacerbate the fear of death. At the same time, the fear of death can trigger depression, as the individual may feel they have limited control over their mortality.

Research has shown that people with an intense fear of death may be more likely to experience depression and that treating the fear of death can lead to a reduction in symptoms of depression.

Treatment for fear of death and depression typically involves a combination of therapy and medication. Cognitive-behavioral therapy (CBT) and exposure therapy can help individuals to confront and manage their fear of death. Drugs such as antidepressants can also be effective in treating depression.

It's important to note that fear of death is a natural feeling, and it's normal to experience it at some point in our lives. It's important to seek help if the fear of death prevents you from living your life fully and is causing significant distress. A mental health professional can help you understand and manage these feelings so that you can live your life to the fullest.

The diagnosis of depression is typically made by a mental health professional, such as a psychiatrist, psychologist, or primary care physician. They will conduct a thorough evaluation, which may include a physical examination, a review of the patient's medical history, and an assessment of the patient's symptoms.

Several tests are commonly used to aid in the diagnosis of depression, including:

1- The Diagnostic and Statistical Manual of Mental Disorders (DSM-5): This manual is used by mental health professionals to diagnose mental disorders, including depression. It provides a set of criteria that must be met for a diagnosis of depression.
The Diagnostic and Statistical Manual of Mental Disorders (DSM-5) is the most widely used diagnostic tool for mental disorders, including depression. It provides a set of criteria that must be met for a diagnosis of depression. The measures include persistent feelings of sadness or loss of interest, changes in appetite or sleep, guilt or worthlessness, and difficulty concentrating.

According to the DSM-5, at least five of these symptoms must be present for at least two weeks for a diagnosis of depression to be made.

2- The Patient Health Questionnaire (PHQ-9): This is a self-administered questionnaire that assesses the severity of symptoms of depression. It is commonly used by primary care physicians to screen for depression and can also be used to monitor treatment progress.

The Patient Health Questionnaire (PHQ-9) is a self-administered questionnaire that assesses the severity of symptoms of depression. It is commonly used by primary care physicians to screen for depression and can also be used to monitor treatment progress. The questionnaire consists of nine questions that assess symptoms of depression, such as feeling hopeless or guilty and difficulty sleeping or concentrating. A score of 10 or higher on the PHQ-9 is considered to be indicative of depression.

3- The Beck Depression Inventory (BDI): This is another self-administered questionnaire that assesses the severity of symptoms of depression. Mental health professionals in the assessment of depression commonly use it.

The Beck Depression Inventory (BDI) is another self-administered questionnaire that assesses the severity of symptoms of depression. Mental health professionals in the assessment of depression commonly use it. It consists of 21 questions that assess symptoms such as sadness or hopelessness, changes in appetite or sleep, and difficulty concentrating. A score of 10 or higher on the BDI is considered to be indicative of depression.

4- The Hamilton Rating Scale for Depression (HRSD): This is a clinician-administered rating scale that assesses the severity of symptoms of depression. It is commonly used in clinical trials to measure the effectiveness of treatments for depression.

The Hamilton Rating Scale for Depression (HRSD) is a clinician-administered rating scale that assesses the severity of symptoms of depression. It is commonly used in clinical trials to measure the effectiveness of treatments for depression. The scale consists of 17 items that assess symptoms such as guilt or worthlessness, changes in appetite or sleep, and difficulty concentrating. A score of 18 or higher on the HRSD is considered to be indicative of depression.

It's worth mentioning that these tests are not meant to be used as standalone diagnostic tools; they are usually used with other information and observations by a mental health professional. A diagnosis of depression is made based on a combination of factors, including the patient's symptoms, medical history, and laboratory test results.

It's important to note that depression is a severe medical condition that requires proper diagnosis and treatment. If you think you may be experiencing symptoms of depression, it's essential to seek help from a mental health professional.

Conclusion

Depression is a severe mental health condition that affects millions of people worldwide. It is characterized by persistent feelings of sadness, hopelessness, and a lack of interest in activities that were once enjoyed. Depression can also manifest as physical symptoms such as changes in appetite or sleep, fatigue, and difficulty concentrating. The condition can range from mild to severe and significantly impact a person's quality of life.

Depression can be classified into several types: major depressive disorder, persistent depressive disorder, and seasonal affective disorder. The causes of depression are complex and can include a combination of genetic, biological, environmental, and psychological factors.

Effective treatment for depression typically involves a combination of therapy and medication. Cognitive-behavioral therapy (CBT) and interpersonal therapy (IPT) are two effective types of therapy in treating depression. Antidepressant medications, such as selective serotonin reuptake inhibitors (SSRIs), may also be prescribed to help alleviate symptoms of depression.

Prevention of depression includes maintaining a healthy lifestyle, regular exercise, getting enough sleep, a nutritious diet, social support, and developing healthy coping mechanisms. It's also important to be aware of the signs and symptoms of depression and to seek help if you or someone you know is struggling.

In conclusion, depression is a severe mental health condition affecting millions worldwide. It is characterized by persistent feelings of sadness, hopelessness, and a lack of interest in activities that were once enjoyed. It can be classified into several different types and significantly impact a person's quality of life. However, with the proper treatment and support, it is possible to manage the symptoms of depression and improve the quality of life. It's essential to seek help if you or someone you know is struggling with depression.

References used " i"

- *Riverhills Neuroscience. https://www.riverhillsneuro.com*

- *National Library of Medicine. https://www.ncbi.nlm.nih.gov*

- *Course Hero, Inc. https://www.coursehero.com*

- *Democrats abroad. https://www.democratsabroad.org*

- *The Substance Abuse and Mental Health Services Administration (SAMHSA) . https://www.samhsa.gov*

- *Institute of Health Metrics and Evaluation. Global Health Data Exchange (GHDx). http://ghdx.healthdata.org*

- *Tsuang MT, Faraone SV. The genetics of mood disorders. Baltimore, MD: Johns Hopkins University Press, 1990.*

- *Cochran SV, Rabinowitz FE. Men and depression: clinical and empirical perspectives. San Diego: Academic Press, 2000.*

- *Gallo JJ, Rabins PV. Depression without sadness: alternative presentations of depression in late life. American Family Physician, 1999;*

- *Lyness JM. Psychiatric disorders in medical practice. In: Goldman L, Schafer AI, eds. Goldman-Cecil Medicine. 26th ed. Philadelphia, PA: Elsevier; 2020:chap 369.*

- *Caroline B Goldberg https://www.carolinebgoldberg.com*

- *CORE THINKING https://corethinking.in*

www.ingramcontent.com/pod-product-compliance
Lightning Source LLC
Chambersburg PA
CBHW061333120726
48001CB00002B/836